WORDS TO BE KEPT IN YOUR POCKET

HARSHITHA NADIKUDA

ISBN 979-888606025-6

Contents

Contents

Preface

The book "Words to be kept in your pocket" aspires to inspire you. It gives an advice about how to live successfully. Through the skillful use of language, I portrayed a few heartening words for you.

This book shall change your superfluous thought pattern. Hence, you'd love thyself a little more and work on your dreams with determination. The negativity would vanish and by uplifting you, for sure.

Acknowledgements

I feel a great sense of gratitude towards God for guiding me through his blessings.

Secondly, I'm pleased to thank Notion press publication house for enabling the creation of this wonderful book.

I would like to thank my parents and all my well-wishers for supporting me.

And finally, I kindly thank the readers in advance for sparing your valuable time to read this book.

Prologue

In our life we may come across many people. Some may be joyous, prosperous, popular, successful and in contrast the other may be poor, miserable, unpopular, unsuccessful. Yet they are perfect in their own way.

As we know, life is a combination of sorrow, misery, disappointment, frustration, failure, cheerfulness, contentment, success, etc. So, receive every moment and grasp something new from these experiences of your life. Uplift thyself for reaching the zenith.

1. AWAKE INGENUITY

For a grand opening of your ideas
Consider this new year as an opportunity
And put forth your thoughts into use
Without any shilly-shally.
Infact, new beginnings are always challenging
Notheless challange those challenges;
Because, warriors are born from those challenges itself.
Life is never free from hassles
You should envision orphic glory by yourself
As none could create the same for you;
For this, don't curb your glee every single time
In lieu, accomplish your objectives by flying in colours.

2. TAKE STEPS FORWARD

Design a regime,
Awake your passion, haunt it,
Lastly, bring to life.

3. EVOLVE, LEARN AND GROW

Burn
Break-downs,
Bloom beyond;
Battles beacons,
Bleed, besides bloom, bind
By bournes between,
Brilliantly,
Become
Best.

4. BEHOLD THYSELF

Awaiting with an air expectancy makes no sense
In lieu, be a smart cookie;
Put on your passion
Along with equanimity
In order to accomplish your objectives
Nevertheless, you fail
If you wanna stick to your passion
Thee had to reincarnate thoughts
With a flawless vision
By absconding all dejections
And let your dreams haunt you
Until you pull off success
You'll envision a transformation in your life
Likewise, an alteration of blank canvas to a magnificent painting
Only if you designate thyself as an artist for your life;
Henceforth you shall sought solace from the epiphany

5. BEAUTY

Towards you, beauty inclines
And shall never decline,
If you wear a pretty smile,
Along with, loving yourself in every mile.

6. FEAR

Fear is that weakness,
Which kills our aspiration.
To achieve your goals,
Just smile at your fears,
Undoubtedly, you can build
A successful career.

7. CHALLENGES

Challenges are important
For the reason that,
They help you,
To know your potential.
If you face the challenges,
You'll know your strength and weakness,
And hence you can put more efforts
To overcome all your weakness.
In this process,
Your life becomes a thrilling one,
Where you come across many experiences.

8. BE YOURSELF

Dear stranger,
Why would you want to be someone,
When you could be better by being yourself?
Why would you pretend to be someone else,
When you've something they haven't got?
Open your eyes,
See the eternal fire within,
Fill yourself with courage,
To perceive your dreams.
Bask in the warmth of light,
By breaking free from cobwebs.
Be hungry to fill the light,
Strive to fulfill your desires,
And fill the aching eyes with sight.
Cast away the darkness,
Dispell all the fears,
Drive away the shadows,
And revitalize your aspirations.

9. PROGRESS WITHOUT BOUNDS

Do what you like, not what others prefer,
Because ideas differ.
Just stop thinking about what others feel,
Since it's your deal.
Build a dream,
And achieve it with an esteem.
You will have your own talent,
Execute it with your own concept.
Convert your dreams into action,
As it's your passion.
Be creative and expressive,
To prove your aptitude.

10. YOU ARE A PHOENIX

When life pushes you down,
Don't loose your hope;
In lieu, revitalize your interests
By bouncing back
Like a phoenix,
Ultimately you shall accomplish your targets.

11. SELF-CONFIDENCE

Inside of you
There's a light
Which leads you,
It is self-confidence.
Sometimes, without switching on the light
People presume to be unfit
Inspite of holding knowledge.
Nevertheless you fail,
Treasure this magical light
It shall lead you
Even in the darkest night.

12. SELF LOVE

Are you searching for true love?
If yes, then immediately stand before a mirror,
You shall find the person
Who shall shower the purest love.
Fall head over heels for yourself
Adorn your beauty,
Praise yourself,
Fill the confidence with-in,
And be in a view that you're enough
If you do so,
Your heart shall never break,
Because you're in love with yourself.

13. IDEALLY BUILD UP YOURSELF

Never think that you're less
Instead, about your dreams, thou discern;
Don't envisage all the mess,
In lieu, do implement your ideas at your turn.
If you fail, try to learn
But never let your goals fall asleep
The deepest knowledge you'll earn
Henceforth the kernels of your dreams will reap.
No one can sweep,
The ambition that you had
If your thoughts turn into action which are in heap;
So, step forward and bloom like a bud.
Don't worry, like the waves, do make your way to the pebble shore
And fulfill your aspirations therefore.

14. HAPPINESS

Happiness is the state of mind,
With-in you, you shall find.
Being happy is a piece of cake
Prima facie it's for your sake
Because you'd live with good health
And hence can avoid early death.

15. VICTORY IN YOUR VEINS

Don't limit yourself,
Explore and grow
Nonetheless you fail
The sunrise is a second chance
Do play hard
Leave all the tragedies behind
Taste the success in one of the subsequent attempts
Because victory is in your veins

16. NEW BEGINNINGS

New beginnings are always challenging,
Even so, hold pendulum of hope,
Inherit thoughts
And tackle all debacles in every move.
Your ideas can put a perfect checkmate
To disintegration,
So, produce lively thoughts
For the purpose of progressing;
Evolve, learn and grow therefore.

17. DEBACLES - A MERE GUEST

Debacles doesn't diminish your aptitude
So, digress from dejection,
Develop self-confidence
As dearth of it could detract you.
Never despair, in lieu develop
Decisive quality, to decode your dreams.
Hold determination in your decorum,
You shall defeat your dilapidated past
To envision a delightful present
And future too.

18. EXPLORE YOURSELF

To attain ascertainity about yourself,
Atleast be audible to your soul.

Prima facie, adore your arcane talent,
And approbate thee ideas.
Assuage yourself in your every thick and thin,
And animate your dreams,
Lastly, you shall become an astute personality.

19. YOU ARE ENOUGH - AN ADORNED TRUTH

Even though you aren't beautiful,
Even if you aren't smart enough,
In spite of not being strong,
Even supposing you aren't perfect,
Yet you're perfect.
Step forward bravely,
Share your esteemed ideas,
Do fail,
Learn from thee mistakes,
And don't forget to love yourself,
You shall lead a delightful life
Because you're enough indeed.

20. SPRING TIME BLOOMS

Do you wanna flee with a mask of glee?
If yes, then would be free from all the hassles?
Running away from problem
Isn't the correct path.
Inspite of getting away,
Fight with them
As a fighter exits with-in thee
Move by move, deliberate that you're smart
And lastly resolve all your complications.
All pages of thee life wouldn't be sad,
Turn your pages,
You shall find glee and peace too.

21. PERSONIFICATION OF HOPE

At a point of time
You would be down-hearted
But none would recognise it.
If you fall into depression
You'll definitely suffer
By drowning into unfruitful thoughts
You shall suffocate and die.
Life is a gift
Peel withers which are surrounded
Cherish the gift
With a smile on your face.

22. HUMANITY

None could stop the evil from rising,
If they're people without humanity.
Being kind and polite
Are the flowers of humanity,
Which are rare to find now-a-days.
Nevertheless you face a worse situation
Keep your humanity alive
And let the people reminiscence your good deeds.
Always do remember that
The entire world will be in a state of peace
If and only if people live in a harmony.
If this element is present with-in you
You shall envision this world as a beautiful palace.

23. SUICIDE

Suicide is not an option,
For you to choose if you feel low.
Don't dare to think in a short-sighted view,
As your passions are in due.
Suicide is not a child's play,
And it's not a correct thought anyway,
As there is another day,
To make a new way.
Never fall on your sword,
Believe in the Lord,
Aim for the best,
God will throw-out the pest.
Life is a war,
You are a star,
Success is not so far,
Then why you'll knock the deaths door?
You're here on the earth for a reason,
So don't build a prison.
You mean a lot to many,
Are you ready to make their hearts heavy?
Suicide is not an option,
For you to choose if you feel down.
Hope for the best in everything,

As you are amazing.

'Rise and Shine'

24. PAINT YOUR RAINBOW

Paint a rainbow in your heart,
Which is radiant and resplendent.
Don't worry if darkness surround thy,
Learn from it and raise high.
At any moment, never feel low,
Instead, happiness seeds you sow,
Coat your rainbow with colours of smiles,
That glows sincerely over the miles.
Dye the rainbow with seven emotions,
And be strong enough to face any hurdle in every motion;
Do all that you can do to achieve your goal,
Then happiness will held in the depths of your soul.
Adorn thou life with colourful days,
Thy days will be bright in all the ways;
Be an author to script all thee experiences,
And be an inspiration.
Sketch a rainbow with your fingers of love,
To design your life like wow!

Thank you for choosing

"WORDS TO BE KEPT IN YOUR POCKET"

9 798886 060256

Printed by Libri Plureos GmbH in Hamburg,
Germany